DinoZone
MEAT-EATING DINOSAURS

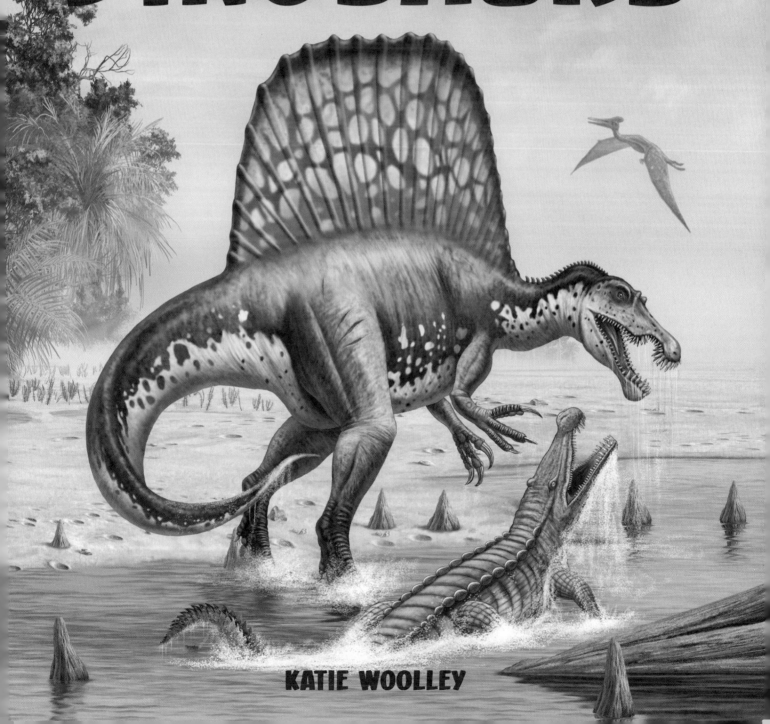

KATIE WOOLLEY

This edition published in 2020 by Arcturus Publishing Limited
26/27 Bickels Yard, 151–153 Bermondsey Street,
London SE1 3HA

Author: Katie Woolley
Designers: Neal Cobourne and Emma Randall
Editors: Joe Harris and Anna Brett

Cover illustration: Rudolf Farkas
Interior illustrations: Arcturus Image Library (Stefano Azzalin: 5, 14, 18,
22l, 23l, 27; Martin Bustamante: 7, 12, 13, 16, 19, 20; Juan Calle: 10, 11,
15, 17, 21, 22r; Liberum Donum: 25; Colin Howard: 26; Kunal Kundu:
9; Val Walerczuk: 4); and Shutterstock: 7, 29 (Key: b-bottom, t-top,
m-middle, l-left, r-right).

ISBN 978-1-83857-259-4
CH008179NT

Supplier: 33, Date 1219, Print run 9718

Printed in China

CONTENTS

Mighty meat-eaters

Meat-eating dinosaurs—the carnivores—were fast-moving, deadly hunters. They had razor-sharp teeth, strong back legs, and hooked claws on the ends of their toes.

Meat-eating dinosaurs lived throughout the Triassic, Jurassic, and Cretaceous periods. *Allosaurus* (AH-loh-SORE-us) lived during the Jurassic period.

Long tail to balance out neck and head

Allosaurus

Big, sharp teeth

Short arms

Claws

Long, strong back legs

4

Acrocanthosaurus (ah-crow-CAN-thoh-SORE-us) was a meat-eater with spines growing out of its back. It lived during the early Cretaceous period.

Most theropods walked on two legs. Theropod means "beast-footed."

Fast Facts

Most meat-eating dinosaurs were theropods (THEH-roh-pods). Some, such as *Allosaurus* and *Acrocanthosaurus*, were huge. Others were tiny.

Acrocanthosaurus

Sharp teeth

Fossilized teeth can help us learn more about dinosaurs. The teeth of a *Tyrannosaurus rex* (tie-RAN-oh-SORE-us REX) were about 23 cm (9 in) long. That's as long as a banana!

Some meat-eating dinosaurs were hunters, while some were scavengers, like modern hyenas. *T. rex* may have been both!

Meat-eating dinosaurs' powerful jaws snapped shut like a crocodile's. Their pointed teeth could pierce flesh and crush bones of bigger prey, such as *Stegosaurus* (STEH-goh-SORE-us). Some meat-eaters had serrated (sawlike) teeth that could rip off chunks of flesh and bone as they ate.

A theropod skull

← A theropod feasting on its prey.

The thorny lizard

The largest meat-eating dinosaur was *Spinosaurus* (SPINE-oh-SORE-us). It was the length of two buses. The spines on its back were covered in skin and looked like a sail. Each spine measured up to 2 m (6.5 ft) high—that's taller than most adults!

The "sail" might have been used to scare enemies or to attract a mate. It could have been used to cool the dinosaur down, too. *Spinosaurus* was possibly the first swimming dinosaur. It spent much of its life in water.

Spinosaurus weighed up to **18 tonnes (20 tons)—as much as 3 elephants!**

Spinosaurus means **"thorn lizard."**

Fast Facts

When: Late Cretaceous period

Food: Other dinosaurs and large fish

Size: 18 m (59 ft) long

→You!

Weight: 4,000 kg (4.4 tons)

How it moved: On two legs

Found in: Egypt and Morocco, Africa

Spinosaurus lived during the Cretaceous period, roaming the swamps of North Africa. It may have eaten dinosaurs, such as sauropods, as well as sharks and other large fish.

A tiny hunter

Hesperonychus (hes-puh-ruh-NIE-kus) was one of the smallest meat-eating dinosaurs that ever lived in North America. It was about the size of a pet cat. It was a deadly predator, although its prey was much smaller than *T. rex's*!

This tiny meat-eater ran on two legs and had an enlarged claw on its second toe. It probably hunted for food such as insects and small mammals. Forests and marshes were its hunting grounds.

Hesperonychus means "western claw."

Fast Facts

When: Late Cretaceous period

Food: Probably insects and small mammals

Size: About 60 cm (24 in) long

← You!

Weight: 1.9 kg (4 lb)

How it moved: On two legs

Found in: North America

Hesperonychus weighed about as much as a chicken.

Hesperonychus may have had feathered wings that helped it glide from tree to tree. This way, it avoided larger predators on the ground.

Lone hunters or pack killers?

Some meat-eating dinosaurs hunted on their own, like tigers and bears. Others hunted in a pack, like wolves. We know this from fossils that show them living alone or in groups.

Yangchuanosaurus (yang-choo-AN-oh-SORE-us) was 10 m (32 ft) long—that's the length of two cars. But it may still have stalked its prey in packs.

Mamenchisaurus

Yangchuanosaurus

Pack hunting would have made it easier to overcome larger prey, such as *Mamenchisaurus* (MAH-men-kee-SORE-us).

Fast Facts

Some meat-eaters may have had saliva full of deadly bacteria. One bite could have poisoned and killed a victim!

Eoraptor (EE-oh-rap-tor) was one of the earliest pack hunters. It had large eyes to see prey from far away.

Eoraptors

Fish for dinner?

Suchomimus (SOO-koh-mim-us) was a large dinosaur with a body that was adapted for eating fish. Its long snout and huge claws were perfect for catching its slippery prey.

Suchomimus

Fast Facts

When: Early Cretaceous period

Food: Fish

Size: 10 m (33 ft) long

You!

Weight: 2,000 kg (2.2 tons)

How it moved: On two legs

Found in: United Kingdom and Spain, Europe

Baryonyx (bah-ree-ON-icks) was a fish-eating dinosaur with a jaw like a crocodile's. It probably waded in water, waiting for its dinner to swim by. Then it would use its large thumb claw like a hook, to stab a passing fish.

Baryonyx's teeth had a jagged edge, like a saw. They were curved inward, making it very hard for a fish to escape!

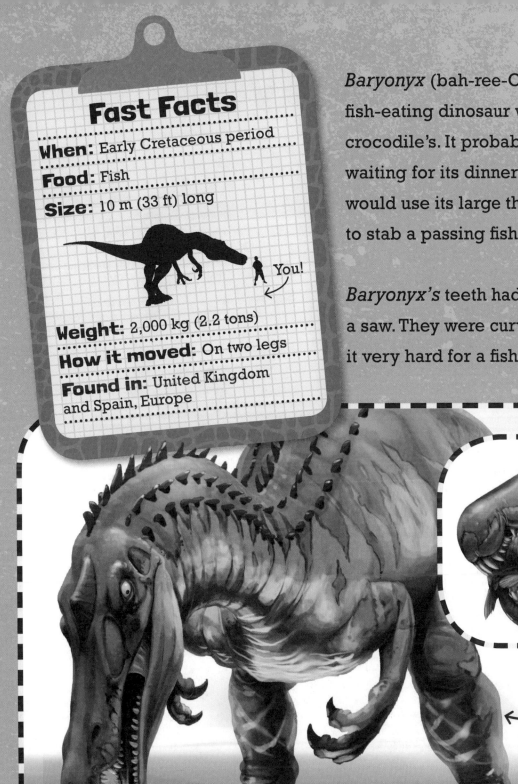

Baryonyx

Baryonyx means **"heavy claw."**

Suchomimus and Baryonyx were related to Spinosaurus.

Small but deadly

Aggressive, light, small, and speedy, *Velociraptor* (veh-LOH-see-rap-tor) was a ferocious predator. It was armed with sharp teeth and claws like daggers. It hunted in packs to catch its prey more easily.

Fast Facts

When: Late Cretaceous period

Food: Other animals

Size: 1.8 m (6 ft) long

You!

Weight: 7–15 kg (15–33 lb)

How it moved: On two legs

Found in: Mongolia, Asia

Velociraptor was the size of a large dog and had strong back legs. It could run at up to 64 km (40 mi) per hour. This meat-eater had 80 teeth and arms with three-fingered claws. It was a fearsome sight!

Velociraptor means "quick plunderer."

Velociraptor lived during the Cretaceous period.

In 1971, a fossil of *Velociraptor* and *Protoceratops* (pro-toe-SEH-rah-tops) locked in combat was found. *Protoceratops* was biting at the arm of the deadly predator, while *Velociraptor* attacked with its claws.

Protoceratops

Velociraptor

Giant southern reptile

Giganotosaurus (jee-gah-NOH-toh-sore-us) was BIG! This massive meat-eater lived 30 million years before *T. rex* came along and was taller and heavier than its more famous cousin. Its teeth were as long as 20 cm (8 in)—bigger than an adult's hand.

At 12.5 m (41 ft) long, *Giganotosaurus* was about the size of a bus. But its brain was only about the size of a banana!

Giganotosaurus means "giant southern lizard."

Fast Facts

When: Early Cretaceous period

Food: Other animals

Size: 12.5 m (41 ft) long

You!

Weight: 4,000 kg (4.4 tons)

How it moved: On two legs

Found in: Argentina, South America

A complete fossil of this dinosaur has never been found. But scientists think *Giganotosaurus* ate large plant-eating dinosaurs, such as *Argentinosaurus*.

Giganotosaurus's sharp teeth had sawlike edges.

Argentinosaurus

Nest-builder

Oviraptor (OH-vee-RAP-tor) was a birdlike dinosaur covered with feathers. Its toothless beak and curved jaws crushed its food. It had a small crest like a horn on its snout. The crest may have been used for mating displays.

Oviraptor was probably an omnivore. It used its tough beak to crush food such as small lizards, fruit, and shellfish.

Oviraptor means "egg thief."

Oviraptor laid its eggs in nests. It sat on the eggs to keep them warm— just like a bird.

Fast Facts

When: Late Cretaceous period

Food: Meat, eggs, insects, shellfish, and plants

Size: 2 m (6.5 ft) long

You!

Weight: 20–30 kg (44–66 lb)

How it moved: On two legs

Found in: Mongolia, Asia

When the fossilized bones of *Oviraptor* were found in the nest of *Protoceratops*, scientists thought that *Oviraptor* was an egg thief. Now, they think the nest belonged to *Oviraptor*, and it was actually looking after its own eggs!

Protoceratops

Oviraptor was about the size of an emu.

Features of hunters

Meat-eaters came in many shapes and sizes. However, they all had some things in common—the features that made them dangerous hunters.

Meat-eating dinosaurs had a powerful sense of smell and good eyesight.

They stood on their toes, and their strong legs helped them to catch prey quickly.

Super senses

Legs made for running

Carcharodontosaurus
(CAR-kah-roh-don-toh-SORE-us)

Dilophosaurus
(dih-LOW-foh-SORE-us)

The skin or feathers of some hunters were patterned to help them blend into the background. This would have helped these mighty meat-eaters to get close to their prey.

Meat-eating dinosaurs were smarter than plant-eaters. They used their intelligence to hunt down other animals.

Brain power

Camouflage

Tarbosaurus
(TAR-bow-SORE-us)

Chindesaurus
(CHIN-dee-SORE-us)

The terrible claw

Deinonychus (die-NOH-nih-kus) was a light and fast-moving dinosaur. It had a hunting claw on each foot. This meat-eater was one of the smartest dinosaurs around—which made it a deadly predator!

Deinonychus was about 3.4 m (11 ft) long—that's twice as big as *Velociraptor*. It hunted in packs. It could use its huge claw to kick and tear its prey apart.

Deinonychus's claw was 12 cm (4.7 in) long!

Fast Facts

When: Early Cretaceous period

Food: Plant-eating dinosaurs

Size: 3 m (10 ft) long

You!

Weight: 75 kg (165 lb)

How it moved: On two legs

Found in: USA, North America

This dinosaur may have been covered in feathers to keep it warm. The feathers also may have been used for mating displays!

Deinonychus means "terrible claw."

Tyrant lizard

Tyrannosaurus rex is the most famous meat-eating dinosaur. With an excellent sense of smell and a fierce appetite, it may not have been the largest, but it was the deadliest beast around.

T. rex's key feature was its huge head and powerful jaws filled with sharp teeth. Its bite could break bones, so it could attack and eat most other dinosaurs. It would even fight rival tyrannosaurs for the chance of a bite to eat.

Its jaws could tear off 230 kg (500 lb) of flesh at one time!

Tyrannosaurus rex means **"tyrant lizard king."**

T. rex had a high IQ, meaning it could plan its attacks on unsuspecting prey.

Fast Facts

When: Late Cretaceous period

Food: Other dinosaurs

Size: 12 m (39 ft) long

Weight: 7,000 kg (7.7 tons)   You!

How it moved: On two legs

Found in: Canada and USA, North America

Meat–eaters around the world

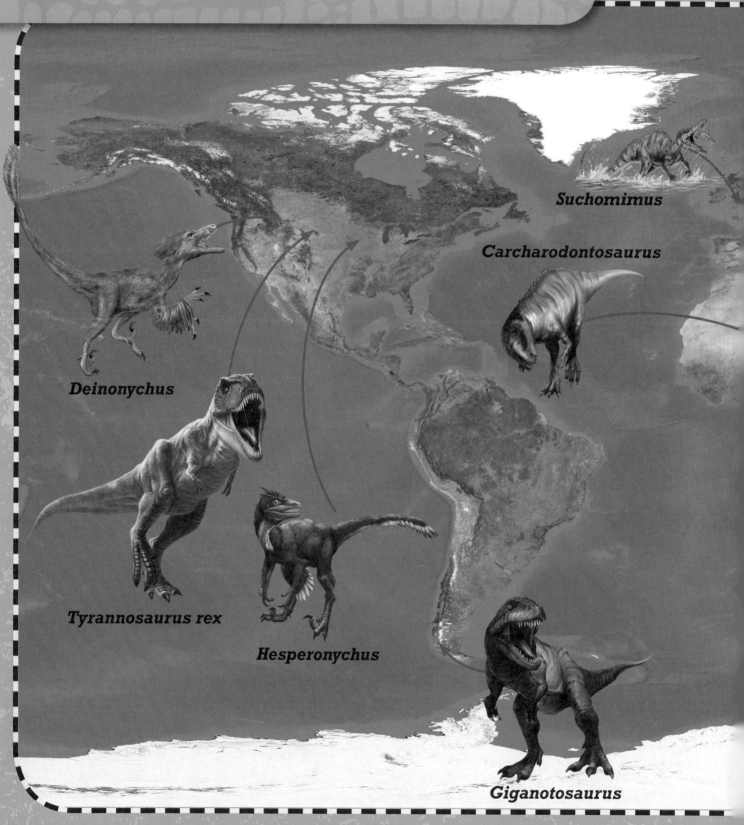

Suchomimus

Carcharodontosaurus

Deinonychus

Tyrannosaurus rex

Hesperonychus

Giganotosaurus

The meat-eaters featured in this book lived all over the world. Can you see one that would have existed near you?

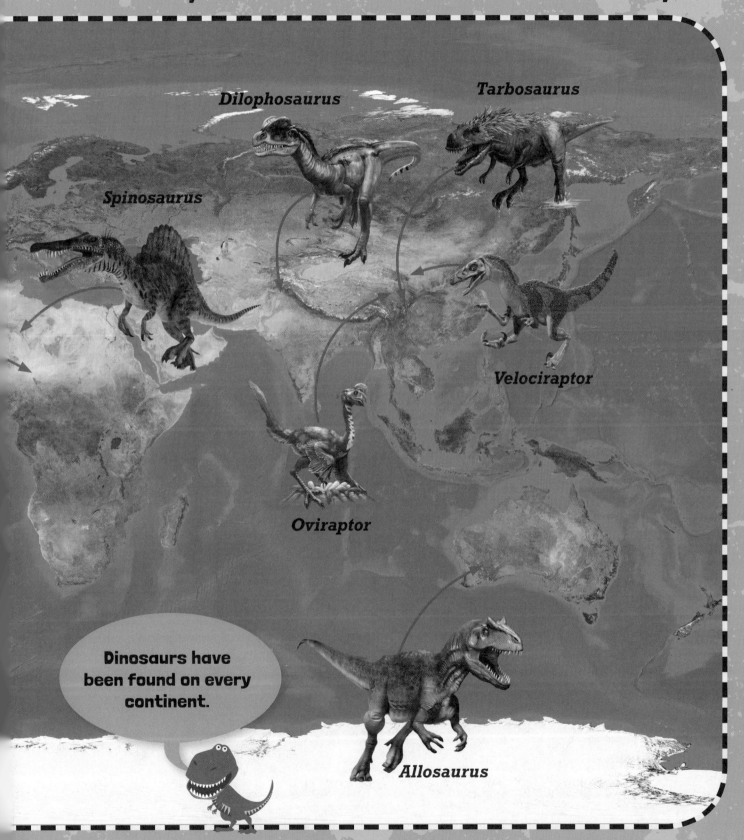

Glossary

adapt Change to new conditions.

appetite A desire to eat food.

camouflage The appearance of an animal that helps it to blend in with its surroundings.

carnivore An animal that feeds on other animals.

crest A comb, tuft of feathers, fur, or skin on the head of an animal.

Cretaceous period A period in Earth's history between 144 and 65 million years ago.

extinct No longer living.

fierce Violent, aggressive, or ferocious.

fossil The remains or imprint of an animal or plant, preserved for millions of years, that has now turned to stone.

frill A fringe of feathers or hair.

glide Move smoothly and continuously.

hunter An animal that searches for and kills its prey.

jagged Rough, sharp edges.

Jurassic period A time in Earth's history between 206 to 144 million years ago.

mate The partner of an animal.

pack A group of animals living together.

predator An animal that eats other animals.

prey An animal that is eaten by other animals.

saliva The watery liquid produced in the mouth to help chewing and swallowing.

sauropods Large, plant-eating dinosaurs with long necks and tails.

scavenger An animal that searches for and collects food.

serrated Having a jagged edge like a saw.

territory An area of land that an animal lives within and defends.

theropods A group of meat-eating dinosaurs.

Triassic period A period in Earth's history between 248 and 206 million years ago.

Further information

Further reading

Beautiful Beasts, A Collection of Creatures Past and Present
by Camilla de la Baedoyaere (Sterling Children's Books, 2015)

The Dinosaur Hunter's Handbook
by Scott Forbes (Carlton Kids, 2015)

Dinosaurs: A Children's Encyclopedia
by editors of DK (Dorling Kindersley, 2011)

National Geographic Kids: The Ultimate Dinopedia
by Don Lessem (National Geographic Society, 2017)

Prehistoric Safari: Giant Dinosaurs
by Liz Miles (Franklin Watts, 2012)

The Usborne World Atlas of Dinosaurs
by Susanna Davidson (Usborne Publishing, 2014)

Websites

http://animals.nationalgeographic.com/animals/prehistoric/
This part of the National Geographic website is home to some fascinating articles about dinosaurs. There are also some excellent pictures.

www.nhm.ac.uk/discover/dino-directory/index.html
The Natural History Museum's Dino Directory is an online guide to these beasts. Content includes facts about over 300 dinosaurs.

www.bbc.com/earth/tags/dinosaur
Articles about dinosaurs on the BBC Earth website. You can find information about origins, discoveries, and record-breakers, as well as videos.

Index